JARGON 101

"This is it. I believe this is sholy it. Yep. This is *good.*" — Roy Blount, Jr.

"What fun! This book makes you want to spit in yer skillet and start cookin' vittles!" — Judith Olney (author of *Joy of Chocolate, Summer Food,* and *Judith Olney's Entertainments*)

"WHITE TRASH COOKING is (dare I say it?) a gas! And coming from the founder of the White Trash Liberation Movement, that's a real compliment!" — Ed McClanahan (author of *The Natural Man* and *Famous People I Have Known*)

"Looking through it, it's clear to me what I am!" — James B. Hunt, Jr., Former Governor of North Carolina

"I'd stop and eat in any of these kitchens, rather than Colonel Sanders or Chez Panisse, for the talk alone." — Ronald Johnson (author of *The American Table, Southwestern Cooking,* and *The Uncookbook*)

"WHITE TRASH COOKING is wonderful. The photographs are a brilliant addition to the recipes. It is the funniest book I have seen in years." — Mark Holburn, Editor, *Aperture*

"How did you know that Trashin Cookin is my favorite of all cuisines? The French and Italians, aside from the peasants, can't begin to compete. I know I shall find many delights in this superb book." — J. William Fulbright, Former U.S. Senator from Arkansas

"Jargon Society, you have did it again, a real pan-fried book, one to harden the arteries just gawkin' at it. The photographs? Almost *eatable.*" — William Least Heat Moon (author of *Blue Highways*)

"That is the most delicious cookbook I have encountered—and it seems my diet in childhood was all White Trash! So many beloved old recipes have turned up. Bless you!" — Helen Hayes

"I enjoyed WHITE TRASH COOKING, it really is amusing reading. But, surely, people don't eat that stuff?" — Athelstan Spilhaus

"I have never seen a sociological document of such beauty—the photographs alone are shattering. I shall treasure it always... Now that it's harder than ever to identify the genuine article on sight—with two generations of prosperity white trash looks like gentry—we've long needed something other than the ballot box to remind us of their presence: WHITE TRASH COOKING is a beautiful testament to a stubborn people of proud and poignant heritage." — Harper Lee (author of *To Kill a Mockingbird*)

"...I read cookbooks like some people read music scores and I can hear the recipes sing! Most of them sound like pretty good eatin'. I *do* like the flavor of this book." — Vertamae Grosvenor ("All Things Considered," *NPR*)

"Perhaps the most intriguing book of the 1986 spring cookbook season is WHITE TRASH COOKING...this book is a delight to peruse. It is one of the few unvarnished regional cookbooks around." — Bryan Miller, *New York Times Book Review*

"You can't beat this book, not even with a Waring blender. It is a great missionary effort, introducing to the hordes of the well-washed such wonders as the Anti-Stick Peanut Butter Sandwich." — Richard Starr, *The Washington Times Magazine*

"WHITE TRASH COOKING is a marvelous and genuine book—not camp—because it sees clearly, without condescension. The food goes from awful with lots of 'oleo' to very good. The language sings throughout." — Barbara Kafka, *Vogue*

SPONSOR TO THE EDITION

CHARLOTTE & PHILIP HANES *(Winston-Salem)*

BENEFACTORS TO THE EDITION

DONALD B. ANDERSON *(Roswell)*

LUCINDA BUNNEN *(Atlanta)*

ANTHONY G. WOOLCOTT *(Key West)*

NATIONAL PATRONS (1984-85) TO THE JARGON SOCIETY

ROY NEILL ACUFF *(Nashville)*

DONALD B. ANDERSON *(Roswell)*

DONALD ANDERSON, JR. *(Casper)*

JOSEPH ANDERSON *(Denver)*

SALLY MIDGETTE ANDERSON *(Roswell)*

SARAH ANDERSON *(Kampsville)*

MARY REYNOLDS BABCOCK FOUNDATION *(Winston-Salem)*

WILLIAM BALFOUR *(Lawrence)*

THE WITTER BYNNER FOUNDATION *(Santa Fe)*

ANNA & THOMAS CHATHAM *(Winston-Salem)*

ROGER CONOVER *(Cambridge)*

W.H. FERRY *(Scarsdale)*

DEWITT CHATHAM HANES *(Winston-Salem)*

ELRIDGE C. HANES *(Winston-Salem)*

F. BORDEN HANES, JR. *(Winston-Salem)*

JAMES G. HANES MEMORIAL FUND/
FOUNDATION *(Winston-Salem)*

JOHN AND ANNA HANES FOUNDATION *(Winston-Salem)*

R. PHILIP HANES, JR. *(Winston-Salem)*

THE HANES COMPANIES *(Winston-Salem)*

"She don't know me from Adam's housecat."
— Nelda Welch, Hot Coffee, Mississippi

WHITE TRASH COOKING

Ernest Matthew Mickler

With Color Photographs by the Author

THE JARGON SOCIETY
TEN SPEED PRESS

Copyright © 1986 by Ernest Matthew Mickler

Library of Congress Catalog Card Number: 85-080302
ISBN: 0-89815-189-9

All Rights Reserved

Design by Jonathan Greene

Decorative cover borders by the author

Setting by *Infotype (Oxford, England)*

Manufactured in the United States of America

Published by:
Ten Speed Press
P O Box 7123
Berkeley, California 94707

25 — 98 97 96

I would like to thank those who gave
me their names as well as their recipes;
and I would also like to thank those who
gave me their recipes without their
names. And a very special thank-you to
John Wayne Keasler of Ball Ground, Georgia;
and Edward Swift of Dime Box, Texas.
E.M.M.

This book is dedicated to
BETTY MAE SWILLEY,
the best cook in Rollin' Fork, Mississippi,
and to ROBERT, who found her
on a tombstone.

CONTENTS

VEGETABLES 'n MEATS (continued)

VEGETABLES 'n MEATS (continued)

FISH, COOTER, 'n SHRIMP   51

DINNER SALADS 'n SWEET SALADS   63

CANDIES, CAKES, COBBLER 'n COOKIES (continued)

SWEET PONES, PUDDINS 'n PIES   97

INTRODUCTION

Never in my whole put-together life could I write down on paper a hard, fast definition of White Trash. Because, for us, as for our southern White Trash cooking, there are no hard and fast rules. We don't like to be hemmed in! But the first thing you've got to understand is that there's white trash and there's White Trash. Manners and pride separate the two. Common white trash has very little in the way of pride, and no manners to speak of, and hardly any respect for anybody or anything. But where I come from in North Florida you never failed to say "yes ma'm" and "no sir," never sat on a made-up bed (or put your hat on it), never opened someone else's icebox, never left food on your plate, never left the table without permission, and never forgot to say "thank you" for the teeniest favor. That's the way the ones before us were raised and that's the way they raised us in the South.

You all know, and we won't let anyone forget it, that the South is legend on top of legend on top of legend. Just read the stories of Eudora Welty, Carson McCullers, William Faulkner, Flannery O'Connor, Truman Capote, and Tennessee Williams. Listen to the songs and stories of Jimmy Rodgers, Mother Maybelle Carter, Hank Williams, Loretta Lynn, Elvis Presley, and Dolly Parton. They all tell us, in their own White Trash ways, that our good times are the best, our bad times are the worst, our tragedies the most extraordinary, our characters the strongest and the weakest, and our humblest meals the most delicious. There ain't much in between. And what really makes us different from others is that we are "in love" with our bad times and weakest characters, we laugh at our worst tragedies, and with a gourmet's delight enjoy our simplest meals. We might tell stories that others think are vulgar or sad, but we make them tales to entertain ourselves and anyone else who will listen. And we always cook enough food for unexpected company. Cooking food, laughing and story telling — that's what we're made of and that's what we enjoy the most.

My mumma died pumping gas at her little filling station/grocery store. Her store was the gathering place. All information, gossip or otherwise, started and stopped at Edna Rae's Grocery Store. If something happened

1

worth gossiping about (and everything was), the store would fill up with people before you could say Jack Robinson. They would all come running out of the palmetto woods, hightailing it for Edna Rae's. She didn't gossip much. She listened and sold groceries and cases of beer and tank upon tank of gas. But in times of misfortune she was always the first to respond. Edna Rae would drag out her cigar box and put a sign on it to collect money for people in need. One sign I clearly remember said, "Please help Iva George and Bertha Sue rebuild their little trailer house. It all burnt down this morning." Then she'd go to the kitchen, and with me to help her she'd cook up a big dinner of fried chittlins, a mess of turnip greens, enough hoe cakes for a Bible story, a wash pot full of swamp cabbage stew, and two large Our Lord's Scripture cakes. Everyone ate in the shade of the shed that covered the gas pumps. When the cigar box was filled to running over with money and all the food was gone, you'd find Iva George and Bertha Sue lazing on the steps of the store, drunk as coots and full as ticks, with lots of company. Bertha Sue's brother, Johnnyboy, saw the trailer burn to the ground. He never talked much until after the fire, but all through dinner he ran around saying, "CRACK and it all burnt down." Mumma said, "He was never really all there." He had some kind of disease when he was a child, and they said, "It eat up part of his brain."

Then there's Big Reba Culpepper, big because there's Little Reba also; Big Reba lives in Burnt Corn, Alabama. She is famous countywide for Reba's Rainbow Icebox Cake. Not too far from Burnt Corn is a place called Flea Hop, Alabama. Big Reba said she has a relative buried "in a small family-type cemetery right out on the edge of town. He was some kind of Civil War hero and when he died he was a very rich man." His grave was richly and clearly marked with a big bronze obelisk "that went way up high," Reba said, "and all his wives (six of them), children, and grandchildren were buried within spittin' distance of his monument. The old cemetery was all growed up with pine trees and needed a whole lot of attention to make it look halfway decent," Reba said. She was afraid if it wasn't cared for someone would steal the big bronze marker. "So I took it on myself to get up a cemetery cleaning party, with rakes, shovels and hoes, fried chicken, Hoppin' John, biscuits, ice tea and, of course, my famous Rainbow Icebox Cake, enough to kill us all. We loaded down the car and took off like Moody's goose for Flea Hop, Alabama." When they reached the cemetery, the marker was gone. She said, "I wasn't at all surprised. That is, until I found it cemented to the ground in front of the Baptist Church. A cousin said he had moved the marker to the church because they needed something pretty out front and great grandpa's marker was the prettiest thing in Flea Hop. "Before, the only thing they had in front of the church was an old sign made out of Cocola caps that said, 'Welcome to the Flea Hop Baptist Church.' I couldn't believe they didn't take the body with the marker," she said. "He was embalmed in some kind of special way that was guaranteed for five hundred years. Now they won't even be able to find him." Then Reba let out a high-pitched laugh, slapped her leg, and licked the last bit of Rainbow Icebox Cake from her lips.

So you see, telling stories, laughing, and enjoying good food are all deeply rooted in our southern White Trash background. We'll tell any story to make it funny. And we'll bend over backwards to make a good meal: from cooking cooter (turtle) in its shell, to making Vickie's Stickies, to putting up Blackberry Acid in jars (hoping it'll ferment). But rather than runnin' around willy-nilly telling stories (which I could do all day long), it might be quicker to get to what I mean by White Trash cooking if, as Betty Sue says, we go straight to the kitchen and "get it did."

If you live in the South or have visited there lately, you know that the old White Trash tradition of cooking is still very much alive, especially in the country. This tradition of cooking is different from "Soul Food". White Trash food is not as highly seasoned, except in the coastal areas of South Carolina, Georgia, and North Florida, and along the Gulf coasts of Alabama, Mississippi, Louisiana, and Texas. It's also not as greasy and you don't cook it as long. Of course, there's no denying that Soul Food is a kissin' cousin. All the ingredients are just about the same. But White Trash food, as you'll see by and by, has a great deal more variety.

If someone asked me what sets White Trash cooking aside from other kinds of cooking, I would have to name three of the ingredients: saltmeat, cornmeal, and molasses. Every vegetable eaten is seasoned with saltmeat, bacon, or ham. Cornbread, made with pure cornmeal, is a must with every meal, especially if there's pot liquor. It's also good between meals with a tall glass of cold buttermilk. And many foods are rolled in cornmeal before they are fried. Of course nothing makes cornbread better than a spoon or two of bacon drippings and molasses. For the sweetest pies and pones you ever sunk a tooth into, molasses is the one ingredient you can't find a substitute for. And a little bit of it, used on the side, can top off the flavors of most White Trash food, even a day-old biscuit.

After ingredients, equipment is the next most important thing. As I've said before, there are no hard and fast rules. But skillets, dutch ovens, and cornbread pans (all of black cast iron) are the only utensils that give you that real White Trash flavor and golden brown crust — and that's what you're after. And don't be too concerned about keeping them clean. Netty Irene says, "It's no trouble at all! All you gotta do is rench 'em out, wipe 'em out with a dishrag, and put 'em on the fire to dry out all the water. Then tear off a piece of grocery bag and fold it about two inches square. Dab it in grease and smear it round 'n round the bottom and sides 'til they're plenty covered. Let 'em cool and hang 'em on a nail." Netty Irene also said that her mother would never use water on her black iron pots and pans, only dry cornmeal. She'd rub them until they were smooth. She said, "Mamma never threw away the used cornmeal, so she always had another cake of cornbread seasoned and in the makin'." Keep your black iron skillet in a good clean condition; it is as special to these recipes as is the wok to Chinese cooking.

Another real common feature of White Trash cooking that sticks out in my mind is that the recipes, because of their deliciousness are swapped and passed around like a good piece of juicy gossip, and by the time they make it back to their source they might be, and almost always are, completely different. Raenelle, Betty Sue's sister-in-law, says, "If I fry down three onions, she's gonna fry down four. If I put in one pack of Jello, she's gonna tump in two." So with every cook trying to outdo the other one, and with all the different tastes, these recipes change so fast it's hard at times to catch them still long enough to get them down on paper. I relied on old family cookbooks, yellowed letters, whispered secrets, and a lot of good hints straight from the kitchens of longtime southern cooks. But I have not written down the endless variations and elaborations on a single dish. And I have not revised the collected recipes unless I had to clarify a very confused situation — and there were a few.

I know you'll lay down and scream when you taste Loretta's Chicken Delight. And Tutti's Fruited Porkettes are fit for the table of a queen. Just how can you miss with a dessert that calls for twenty-three Ritz crackers? And then, there are recipes for coon, possum, and alligator.

These ingredients can even be found in New York City, if you've got an hour and a good taxi driver. You'll be the talk of your social club or sewing circle when you prepare a Resurrection Cake that's guaranteed to resurrect when you pour on the whiskey sauce, or a Grand Canyon Cake or Water Lily Pie that, all going well, look just like their namesakes.

It's not hard to catch on to our ways. Even an awful cook will soon sop them up and become deathly accurate with the sweet potato pones and Miss Bill's Bucket Dumplins. How? No hard, fast rules. Soon you'll find out like the best of the White Trash cooks that there are many ways to fix the same thing, and before long you'll be preparing these dishes with your eyes closed, with the very basics of southern cooking just at your fingertips. I know you'll want to place this cookbook next to the Holy Bible on your coffee table (I know you've got a coffee table with Polaroid snapshots under the glass). And in the kitchen you'll become another Mrs. Betty Sue Swilley, in the true spirit of WHITE TRASH COOKING.

ERNEST MATTHEW MICKLER

ON SERVINGS PER RECIPE

A dear friend of mine, Netta Porter Easterdale, claims to be an expert on portions. She said "All I gotta do is quote my mama." "You take what you've got in the pot and divide it by the number of people you've got to feed or if you only have enough for four everytime another person walks in the door you just add whatever you got the most of to the pot. And it was usually water."

Netta agreed that most of these recipes are for four. "Unless someone tells you different," she said.

Vegetables 'n Meats

UNCLE WILLIE'S SWAMP CABBAGE STEW

1 medium swamp cabbage	2 large chopped onions
3 pieces of fatback	1 teaspoon of white sugar
2 cans of tomatoes	1 pod of hot green pepper,
pinch of thyme	chopped up

Fry fatback, onions, and chopped swamp cabbage til starting to brown. Add tomatoes, sugar, pepper, and thyme. Simmer til it thickens and tomatoes cook down. Add another pinch of thyme 10 minutes before it's done. Serve on rice.

If you don't live along the Carolina, Georgia, North Florida coast, Hearts of Palm in a can will work. But don't cook them too long.

STEWED CABBAGE

1 head of cabbage	3 – 4 slices of fatback or a
	cup of Virginia
	smoked ham chunks

Cut up cabbage into quarters, then break the quarters up with your hands. Fry down the meat in a cast-iron dutch oven. Now put cabbage in the pot and fry it down about 10 minutes (turning often). Salt and pepper to taste and add 1 cup of water. Bring it to a boil and then put on the lid and cook 20 minutes on medium low heat or 35 minutes if you like it gray.

Aunt Bertie Mack says you can't cook a good stewed cabbage unless you know how to sing:

> Boil that cabbage down boy, boil that cabbage down
> Bat your eyes til the crick done rise,
> But boil that cabbage down!

BUTTER BEANS (FRESH)

1 quart of fresh butter beans	¼ lb. of bacon, salt meat, or ham

Fry your meat in a pot until it's brown. Pour in the butter beans and add enough water to come up to the top of the beans but not over. Salt and pepper and cook until the beans are tender and the liquid is reduced to half. Serve on rice with pepper vinegar.

3 lbs. of beans in the shells will give about 1 quart shelled and serves 6. The following list of peas can be cooked just like these beans:
Crowders
Purple-hulls
Field Peas
Lady Cream Peas (good luck trying to find them)

CREAMED ENGLISH PEAS

Add to canned sweet peas the Yankee Tomato Cream Gravy on page 48. Heat together for 10 minutes and serve with fried chicken or chicken-fried steak.

HOPPIN' JOHN

Cook enough black-eyed peas with hog jowls until they are tender. Cook a cup of rice for every 2 or 3 hungry people. Stir the rice and peas together and serve. Some folks put in tomatoes and some put in okra but no matter what you put, anything with peas and rice is going to be called its old White Trash name of Hoppin' John.

Always eaten on New Year's Day, and the more you eat the more good luck you are going to have. "That's common knowledge," says Kaye Kay. She also said: "You can make it out of crowder, field or cow peas."

LIMPIN' SUSIE

1 medium onion chopped
3 cups of sliced okra
½ cup of bacon or ham
    chopped

Fry down the seasoning meat, onion, and okra. Get one cup of rice cooking in another pot and when it is half done add the okra and finish cooking. It'll just cook away to nothing.

MATTY MEADE'S CORN AND TOMATOES

1 part whole canned
    tomatoes
1 part whole canned
    kernel corn

½ small onion chopped
    fine
bacon crumbs

Tump together. Simmer til onion is done. Put in a bowl and serve.
    "If you don't like canned vegetables but it's all you got, put a spoon of vinegar in them while they're cookin. Add salt and pepper and a spoon of bacon grease. It'll make 'em almost good as home-canned." *Mrs. Lulamae Bennett, Starke, Florida.*

INDIAN SUCCOTASH

1 pound can green lima
    beans or two cups
    drained
1 tablespoon oleo

1 12 oz. can whole-kernel
    corn, or 1 ½ cups
    drained
½ cup light cream

Combine, season, and heat.
    Eat with soda crackers spread with mayonnaise.

SUCCOTASH

1 cup fresh corn (cooked)	⅓ cup of salt meat or bacon
1 cup fresh lima or	chopped
butterbeans	⅓ cup onions (chopped)
1 cup fresh cooked	
tomatoes	

Fry meat. Mix everything together. Add enough water to cover the bottom of the pot. Bring to a boil and serve. Canned is passable, if you've never had the real thing.

CORN ON THE COB

Don't shuck your corn until *just* before you get ready to cook it. Take off the husks, the hairs, and cut off the ends. Rinse it off in fresh water and drop into a big pot of fast boiling water (unsalted). Make sure the water covers all the ears. Wait til your water starts to boil again, then turn off immediately and put on the lid so the flavor won't excape. Now let it sit in the hot water for 5 – 10 minutes (5 for young corn). Drain it and salt it, butter it and eat it.

Mrs. Johnny Keasler of Ball Ground, Georgia, says: "It's the only way to cook your corn on the cob."

CORN OFF THE COB

2 cups of fresh corn or	2 tablespoons of butter or
canned	bacon grease
	salt and pepper

In a skillet, heat the oil and put the corn in to fry. Stir it until it has browned a little. Salt, pepper and serve.

You can add cream (canned or fresh) and corn starch or flour to thicken this if you want to.

You can also add a cup of stewed tomatoes instead of the cream and cook it down.

BAKED SWEET POTATO

Select plump, smooth potatoes. Wash 'em and grease 'em. Put in the oven at 350 degrees for 45 minutes or an hour. They should be soft, through and through, when poked with a fork. Serve hot with butter, make pies or pones or just eat them cold. You can't go wrong.

BOILED PEANUTS

If they're green: put them in a pot, add water to cover and much too much salt. Boil 2 or 3 hours until the hardest ones are tender. Eat 'em as a snack. If they're dried: put them in a pot of water and bring them to a boil. Cut off the fire and let them stand overnight or at least 6 – 8 hours. Then boil in salted water for 4 to 5 hours, until the nut inside the shell is tender. Sometimes you can find them put up in cans in the grocery store.

CHARLYSS'S BLACK-EYED PEAS
(OR, WHOLE-GRAINED CORN)

Get yourself a good, non-stick cooking pot and put it over a medium flame. Put in 5 or 6 good heaping tablespoons full of olive oil and allow to heat for a few minutes (2 or 3). Chop up 2 (or 3) good-sized onions and put into the pot. Stir slowly and thoroughly, being careful to mix in a healthy one-half handful of chopped parsley a few minutes after you've added the onions to the pot. Continue to sauté these ingredients for 2 to 3 minutes; then cover and lower flame to slightly under medium. Every 4 to 5 minutes lift the pot cover and stir slowly. While the onions and parsley are cooking slowly, chop about 3 cups full of ham (or thick bacon bits) and add to pot, carefully stirring everything together thoroughly. Open 3 large cans of black-eyed peas. After the onions, parsley and ham pieces have been cooking for about 10 – 15 minutes, add all

3 cans of peas to the pot, stir thoroughly, cover, and cook over a medium flame for about 30 to 45 minutes until tender. Then serve over freshly cooked rice. Serves 3 or 4 hungry people.

Charlyss, the cook and owner of the Side Board Restaurant in Cut-off, Louisiana, feeds a lot of very hungry men. And they keep coming back. "They say it's the only place where you can get filled up and satisfied too."

BONNIE'S BLACK-EYED PEAS

1¼ cups of dried black-eyed peas	1 cup chopped salt pork or fatback
4 cups of water	1 medium onion (chopped)

Put together in pot and cook 3 hours or more (boil slowly). When they are soft, remove one cup and mash well and return them to the pot and salt and pepper to taste. Serve over boiled rice with greens and a meat. Some people enjoy cut-up raw onions and pepper vinegar sprinkled over the top of the peas.

With the leftovers you can make a real quick Hoppin' John by mixing the leftover peas and meat with the leftover rice. Heat and serve for another meal. In Louisiana they call this a Jambalaya.

RED BEANS & RICE

2 lbs. dried red beans (kidney)	1 bunch parsley (chopped)
2 cups chopped yellow onions	3 lbs. of a good smoked sausage cut into 2 inch lengths (smoked ham or ham bone works fine)
1 bunch of scallions (green onions), chopped	salt and pepper to taste
3 – 4 finely sliced cloves of garlic	3 quarts of cold water

Soak beans overnight if possible. Drain water and add beans to a large 8 – 10 quart pot. Then add enough of the cold water to cover the beans. Add chopped yellow onions and garlic and bring to a boil. Cook one hour and add all the other things and more water if necessary. Simmer (slight bubbling action) for 2 more hours or until beans are soft. Then remove 2 cups of cooked beans without juice and mash very good. Then return the mashed up beans to the pot and stir into the mixture. This makes a creamy, thicker gravy. If the beans are too dry, add enough water to make them like you like them. Good over boiled rice. Serves 8.

If you're in New Orleans on Monday, this is the only thing you can eat.

SNAP BEANS

String and snap 2 lbs. of green beans into 1½ inch pieces. Put in a pot with fatback (bacon) or ham hocks. Add a double handful of little new potatoes or 3 to 4 medium ones cut into quarters. Now cover with water, add salt and pepper to taste and cook on a medium-slow fire until the beans are tender and the liquid has cooked down to half.

THE DUTCHESS'S BAKED BEANS
(by Gloria de Long)

3 cups home-cooked beans of any kind (3 cups of Campbell's pork 'n beans will do in a pinch)
1 cup chopped onions

½ teaspoon cinnamon
1 cup ketchup
enough bacon slices to cover the top

Put your beans in a bowl. Mix everything together except bacon slices. Salt and pepper to taste, pour out into a flat baking dish or pan. Cover top with bacon slices and stick it in a 350-degree oven for 35 minutes, or until some of the juice is gone. That's it.

For cooking white beans (Navy, Greater Northern, Lima and others)

1 1 lb. sack of beans	2 quarts of water
1 big ham hock (or picnic ham bone with a little meat left on it)	salt and pepper (as much as you want)
1 big yellow onion chopped	

Some people add a spoon of sugar, soda, or nutmeg.

Put your beans, water and ham hock in a pot. Bring your water to a rolling boil. Turn the fire down to low. Let 'em cook for two and a half hours or until when you mash 'em up they're tender.

If you need to add water, always make sure it's hot. All Cajuns add a handful of chopped green onions and chopped parsley 20 minutes before beans are done. (For shorter cooking time, soak them overnight.)

BETTY SUE'S FRIED OKRA

1 lb. of fresh okra or 2 packages of frozen (cut in rounds)	1½ cups corn meal or cracker meal salt, pepper (heavy salt)

Salt and pepper okra, then shake it in a brown paper sack with 1½ cups of meal til okra is all covered. Heat skillet very hot with ⅓ cup of oil. Put in okra and fry to golden brown (12 minutes or thereabout). Remove from skillet and lay okra on paper towel to absorb excess oil. Serve hot. Enough for 4.

"Steer clear of all those fancy frozen packages of this-in-a-sack or that-in-a-sack. Loose frozen vegetables are just as good, but make sure you season them like you like them," says Mrs. Swilley.

BETTY SUE'S SISTER-IN-LAW'S FRIED EGGPLANT

Wash eggplant in cold water and then peel. Cut it up into round slices ½ inch thick. Dip it in a mixture of 1 egg and ½ cup of milk, and then dredge it in salted-and-peppered cracker meal. Fry in a heavy frying pan in a light oil until golden on both sides. 3 – 4 persons per large eggplant.

If you don't have cracker meal, use corn meal. If you don't have corn meal, use flour.

FRIED CUCUMBER

2 large cucumbers (cut length-wise)	salt
1½ cups of corn meal	pepper

Salt and pepper the cucumbers. Shake in a brown paper sack with 1 ½ cups of corn meal until the cucumbers are covered. Heat ⅓ cup of oil in a very hot skillet. Add cucumbers and fry until golden brown. Remove cucumbers and put on a paper towel to absorb excess oil.

Serves 4 or 5.

FRIED SQUASH

3 large zucchini (cut into rounds)	1½ cups of corn meal

Cook the same as fried okra and cucumbers.

HOME FRIES

1 medium-to-large potato for each person you're serving. Peel and slice them into rounds ⅛ inch thick.

In an iron frying pan heat ¼ or ½ inch of grease until it begins to bubble. Now add your potatoes until they cover the bottom of the pan. Fry on both sides until medium golden-brown. Drain them on paper towels. Salt and serve.

For *French Fries*, cut into sticks and fry as you do Home Fries.

MINDA LYNN'S COLD POTATO SALAD

5 – 7 potatoes cubed and boiled	2 – 3 great big sour pickles all chopped up
½ cup mayo (sometimes more is best)	several hard-boiled eggs all chopped up (5 will
¼ cup onion all chopped up	do, but 8 make a richer salad)
1 teaspoon mustard (sometimes more, sometimes less)	pickle juice to taste
	salt to taste
	pepper to taste

Put all ingredients together in a big pan and mix it up. If you need more moisture, add more pickle juice, or a little bit of milk, or mayonnaise. If you need more onion, chop it up and put it in. If you need more pickles, put them in too, but remember they're hard to take out. Some people like more mustard than mayonnaise and a whole lot of eggs. Then it's real, real yellow. Some people like more mayonnaise than mustard and then it's not quite so tart.

Minda Lynn swears you can do anything you want to with this salad, depending on your mood. But she advises to always take the skins off your potatoes because, if you leave them on, the salad will look awfully dirty.

SPUDS HOT POTATO SALAD

4 – 5 large potatoes
½ cup of can cream
2 large spoons of Blue
    Plate mayonnaise
3 large eggs, hard-boiled
2 heaping teaspoons of
    French's mustard

1 medium onion cut up
    in thin pieces
salt and black pepper
    to taste

Peel potatoes and cube in large pieces. Put in pot and boil until they're soft through and through. (You can boil your eggs with the potatoes if you want to.) When potatoes are soft, drain the water and then mash like mashed potatoes. Set aside. Cut up onion and cut up eggs. Add them to the potatoes along with cream, mayonnaise, mustard, salt, and black pepper. Mix thoroughly and serve hot.

    This recipe is from Spuds, Florida. According to Mrs. Myrtle Batten it's the potato capital of the world.

JOLLEY'S SCALLOPED TATERS

6 medium potatoes sliced
3 medium onions sliced
1 stick of oleo
    salt and pepper to taste

1 can of Pet milk and
    enough water to make it
    2 cups

Parboil the onions and potatoes for 10 minutes and drain. Put in a dish or a pan you can bake in. Put the oleo on the potatoes and onions while they hot so it'll melt all down. Then cover them with the milk and don't forget to salt and pepper. Put in a medium oven (350 degrees) for 30 or 40 minutes until they're good and brown. This should feed 5 or 6 at dinner time.

MAMMY'S MASHED POTATOES

Peel 4 or 5 medium-to-large potatoes and dice into ½ to 1 inch cubes. Boil in just enough water to cover them up and throw in a teaspoon of salt to bring out the flavor. When forked and they're tender all the way through (30 minutes usually), drain off the water, then mash them up with your masher until there are no more lumps. Add a tablespoon of butter and two tablespoons of cream (canned or other). Serve hot with brown gravy.

MAMMY'S COLORED MASHED POTATOES

Boil ½ lb. carrots (3 or 4) and ½ lb. potatoes. Mash potatoes and carrots together and follow Mammy's Mashed Potato recipe. They look so pretty and bright the children will love them and grown-ups too.

There are many potato mashers on the market but, according to Mammy, the best one there is is a quart fruit jar. "The bottom's not too large and not too small. Mashes 'em up real good."

EDNA RAE'S SMOTHERED POTATOES

4 medium potatoes, sliced in rounds ¼ inch thick
1 onion, or 1 bunch of scallions, chopped

red pepper
salt

Fry onions in cast-iron skillet in 2 tablespoons of bacon grease or other cooking oils until limp and kind of brown. Add potatoes and stir til all of them are covered in oil and starting to brown. Add 1 cup of water, salt, and pepper. Put lid on and cook til potatoes are soft and brown in some places. Then add green onions and red pepper and cook 10 minutes more. Serve with pork or fried chicken.

"Let them get a real brown crust on bottom without burnin', that's the trick," Edna Rae says.

NETTY IRENE'S MACARONI & CHEESE

4 cups cooked elbow
  macaroni
1 cup grated or chunked
  yellow cheese
3 eggs
1 cup Carnation evaporated
  milk (no substitute,
  please)

10 bacon strips (or enough
  to cover)
salt and pepper

Blend the eggs and milk together and pour into macaroni already in a flat pyrex baking dish. Put in the cheese and poke it around until thoroughly mixed. Salt it to taste. Then put enough black pepper to coat it all real good. Place on bacon slices and cook in 350-degree oven until it gets a good crust on top and has hardened a little. About 30 – 40 minutes. Don't cook it too long, you want it runny in between the elbows.

"This recipe is from Miss Myrtle Talmadge's Home-Ec class and I made it for the Senior Prom Dinner. It was so good I been makin' it ever since," Netty told me.

ONION PIE

½ stick oleo, melted

2 large onions, chopped up

Fry onions in oleo until limp, but don't brown. Let 'em cool slightly and add 1 tablespoon flour, ⅓ can evaporated milk, ⅛ teaspoon salt and one cup of sweet milk. Cook all above ingredients until thick. Beat three eggs in a bowl and add to mixture. Pour into 9-inch unbaked pie-shell. Top with another pie-shell. Brush with milk. Bake at 425 degrees for 30 – 40 minutes.

Serve with Ham-Lima Salad found on page 65.

MIKE MITCHELL'S GRANDMOTHER'S SPINACH PIE

1 lb. or bunch of fresh
    spinach or
1 lb. can of spinach,
    drained
2 eggs
2 tablespoons of chopped
    onion/green scallions
2 tablespoons of evaporated
    milk

4 oz. sharp cheddar cheese
salt and pepper
2 pie crusts (one for pan
    and other for top)
2 tablespoons of butter

Fresh spinach: Fry spinach and onion in the butter til onions are transparent and spinach wilted.
Canned spinach: Fry onions and add spinach.

Beat eggs and milk with a fork and add to spinach and onions. Put in an uncooked pie-shell and cover the spinach mixture with the slices of cheese ¼ inch thick. Then put the other pie crust on top and bake for 15 or 25 minutes (or until top is brown) at 350 degrees.

Serve hot. Enough for 6.

MARY BETH BONEY'S COLLARD GREENS

Wash your collards 3 or 4 times in fresh water, draining them each time. (There's nothing worse than gritty collards.) Then strip the leafy part from the stems and throw the stems to the chickens, if you got any. In a large pot fry down 1 lb. of fatback, thick bacon, or ham chunks til brown. Then add collards. Stir and fry all this until collards start to wilt. Add 2 cups of water and cook until tender. Add more water if necessary. Some people like a spoon of sugar in the water to sweeten the greens. Stir frequently on medium heat so they don't burn.

OLETA BROWN'S TURNIP GREENS

Manage the same as collards, but you can add the turnip bottoms to the greens for cooking. Just peel them and cut them into 2-inch chunks. Delicious with black-eyed peas, ham hocks, and corn bread.

MUSTARD GREENS

Manage the same as collards but cooking time is shorter (usually).

Coleta Davis always cooks her mustard, collards and turnips together in one big pot and seasoned with bacon fat.

TANYA (ELEPHANT EARS)

Pare the tanya root as you would a turnip. Cook in saucepan with cold water and bring to a boil. Pour the water off, add more cold water and a little salt, and cook until tender. Slice and serve hot with drawn butter.

CRÊPES À LA CREOLA LE BEAU

1 can Campbell's Cream
  of Mushroom Soup
½ cup mayonnaise
  collard greens (left-over
  collards are best)

crêpes (go buy a package
  of flour tortillas)

Cook soup (DO NOT THIN) and mayonnaise til hot. Fill crêpes with left-over collards. Pour the sauce over them and serve.

COLD COLLARD SANDWICH

Use enough ice-cold, left-over collard greens to cover a slice of light bread. Sprinkle on some pepper vinegar to taste. Then cover the other slice of bread generously with Blue Plate mayonnaise and eat.

    This is truly a southern delicacy since there are seldom any collards left.

MARY LINDER'S WASHDAY SOUP

Put Navy beans in a big pot of salted water to soak overnight. Put on with the wash water about six in the morning, with bacon, or ham. Let cook uncovered on low burner. Clock between loads of wash. Add 1 large, finely minced onion at eight when you're blueing the overalls. At nine have a quick cup of coffee and dump ½ cup in the beans if you want. Add ½ cup fine minced carrots at bleach time (about eleven). Serve at noon with soda crackers and slaw you made the night before. For washday this is a pretty good deal.

HOMEMADE VEGETABLE SOUP

1 cup corn	1 beef soup bone
1 cup green beans	1 cup of stew meat (beef)
1 can stewed tomatoes	2 toes of garlic
2 cups of potatoes (cut up)	salt and black pepper or
2 cups of yellow onions	Tabasco® to taste
(cut up)	

Put everything in a soup pot and cover with water (about 2 inches over the vegetables). Cook until meat and vegetables are falling apart. Add 1 bunch of green onions (chopped), ½ bunch of parsley (chopped). Cook 20 minutes more and taste of it to see if it's ready to serve. Soda crackers or cornbread?

MOCK COOTER STEW

1½ lbs. of ground lean pork
1½ lbs. of ground lean beef
4 cups water
   salt and pepper
1 stick of oleo
3 cups of milk

1 cup of canned cream
   double pinch of dried
   mustard
2 tablespoons of flour
4 hard-boiled egg yolks
   chopped up into hunks

Cook the meat in the water, salt and pepper. When it's tender add the oleo, milk, canned cream and mustard. Bring back up to hot but do not *boil*. Put in 2 tablespoons of flour and cook until thick. Add egg yolks and serve. Refer to the cooter section for the real thing.

   Mrs. Ina Filker of Sandfly, Georgia, says: "Give you a silver dollar if you kin tell the difference."

PORE FOLK SOUP

For a light supper, crumble soda crackers in warm milk. Salt, pepper, and eat with a spoon.

Hooka tooka my soda crackers?
Does yer Mammy chaw tobaccer?
If yer Mammy chaw tobaccer then
Then Hooka tooka my soda cracker?

BRENDA'S BLACK BEAN SOUP

3 cups of dried black beans
2 ham hocks
1 bell pepper (chopped)
1 small onion (chopped)
1 whole sour orange or
   tangerine

1 tablespoon vinegar (if you
   use a sweet orange or
   tangerine)
1 stick of oleo
2 tablespoons of flour
   salt and pepper to taste

Put your beans in a soup pot and cover with water. Boil, take off the fire and let sit til cool. Cook onions and bell peppers in ½ the oleo until limp. Add them and the ham hocks and orange to the cooled beans; cover charitably with water. Simmer until the beans is soft (1 to 2 hours). Fish out the orange right now, before it gets tore up. With the rest of the oleo, brown the flour in a black frying pan, then stir it into the beans. Brenda says: "Make sure you got a soup, now. If you need to add some more water, do it."

MRS. HENRY DORSEY SHORT'S REAL COUNTRY-SMOKED HAM

1. Soak in water overnight (covered).
2. Scrub.
3. Put in roaster with:
     6 cups water
     1 cup bourbon
     1 handful sugar.
Simmer until you can wiggle the bone.

PORK ROAST

Take a sharp knife and stick holes in the roast and stuff each hole with a sliver of garlic. The holes should be about 1½ – 2 inches apart. Then rub the roast with lots of salt, pepper and a little brown sugar. Have your dutch oven on the stove with just enough grease to brown the roast on all sides. Surround it with sweet potatoes (whole). Cover it and cook slowly until the pork is tender and *well done*. If you need some juice, use a little water.

   Some people brown their pork roast on top of the stove and then put it in the oven. It takes a little longer but they say it's better.

PORK CHOPS

Cut the excess fat off the chops. Salt and pepper them. Douse them in flour and fry in hot grease over medium heat until they're golden brown and *well done*, but not dry.

   Make gravy from the drippins (page 47).

   Make sure you look after the pork chops with some good Motts apple sauce or pickled apples.

TUTTI'S FRUITED PORKETTES

1 pound sweet potatoes	6 tender pork chops
12 slices canned pineapple	6 tablespoons brown
6 slices bacon, cut into	sugar
halves	

Select sweet potatoes to make slices a bit smaller than pineapple slices. Cut into slices 1 inch thick. Parboil the potatoes in salted water for 10 minutes. Place each chop between two slices of pineapple. Place slice of sweet potato on top of each pork-pineapple stack. Sprinkle each porkette with one tablespoon of brown sugar. Place bacon crisscross on top. Place porkettes in open casserole. Bake at 375 degrees for one hour or longer, depending on thickness of chops.

Tutti, Petie's grandma, said "she learned to make her porkettes by using a Hawaiian recipe combined with Southern ingredients. You cain't git trashier than that."

SAUERKRAUT & SPARERIBS

1 large can sauerkraut	2 lbs. spareribs
(drained)	

Get the butcher to chop the spareribs into 2 – 3 inch links. Salt and pepper them. Then in a heavy bottom pot, heat ⅛ inch grease and brown the spareribs on all sides. Add sauerkraut, cover and cook until the ribs are tender and coming off the bone. Serve with Mammy's Mashed Potatoes.

SINGLE BOY'S BREAKFAST

Take one pound of pork sausages. Cook them evenly, pour off fat. Add one and one half box soda crackers (unsalted) crumbled. Pour in one cup of boiling water. Cover tight and steam five minutes. Serve with fried sweet potatoes and plenty of hot, black coffee.

FRESH FRIED SWEET POTATOES

Peel and slice the sweet potatoes lengthwise and place immediately in a heated iron frying pan with ¼ inch of grease. Fry until golden brown and soft in the middle when poked by a fork. Goes good with sausage or bacon.

NOBODY'S CORN TOPPER CASSEROLE

(made with ham)

1 1 pound can cut green beans, drained	4 tablespoons finely-chopped onion
1 can cream of mushroom soup	2 cups cubed cooked ham
1 1 pound can cream-style corn	¾ cup prepared biscuit mix (Bisquick)

Place beans in a 2-quart greased casserole, reserving a few for garnish. Sprinkle onion on top; spread with soup. Top with a layer of ham. Bake at 425 degrees for 15 to 20 minutes. Combine corn and biscuit mix. Spoon mixture on top of casserole. Bake for 15 – 20 minutes longer. Garnish with rest of beans.

CHICKEN-FRIED STEAK

round steak	pepper
flour	Crisco, or vegetable oil
salt	of your choice

Take a piece of round steak about as big as a slice of bread and twice as thick. Beat it with the back of a knife* until it's thin, scarred and tender. Then sprinkle it with salt, pepper and flour it on both sides. Flour it until it's all white and you can't see a trace of meat anywhere. (You just about can't get too much.) Now you're ready to fry it on both sides in about ½ inch of hot grease.

Chicken-fried steak should always be cooked *well* done.

Serve with white gravy (below) and mashed potatoes, a slab of lettuce, a wedge of tomato, and crisscross the french fries.

*Pearl Brown always used the edge of a real thick saucer to tenderize her steak. "Be careful not to break it," she always said.

WHITE GRAVY (WITH MILK)

To make a good white milk gravy you've gotta have a good eye for measurements. After you fry your chicken or steak, look at the drippins in the pan and try to decide just how much flour and milk you need to thicken it up without getting too much. If you have just fried a good-sized chicken, or several pieces of steak, and you've got a fair amount of drippins in the skillet, then you'll probably use 2 tablespoons of flour with about ¼ cup of milk. Mix it until there're no more lumps and then add it to the drippins and stir over a low flame until thick. If you get your gravy too thick, just water it down some; if it's too thin, add some more flour. Always keep reminding yourself that it takes years of practice to make a good flour gravy. Nobody's perfect right at the very first.

POT ROAST

Heavily salt and pepper the roast on both sides, then flour it. Put it into a hot dutch oven with about ⅛ inch lard. Sear and fry until golden brown on all sides. This seals in the flavor. Cover with carrots, potatoes, and onions (whole or cut up). Put on the lid and cook on a slow fire until meat and vegetables are tender. If the meat does not have enough juice of its own, add a little bit of water.

Remove the meat and use drippins for gravy (page 47).

SMOTHERED LIVER'N ONIONS

Take 1 pound of calves' liver and cut into 3 or 4-inch squares. Salt, pepper and flour it (coat it real good). Fry it in your skillet in ¼ inch of hot grease until it's done (golden brown). Take out the liver and pour off the grease and make gravy (see page 47).

Put your liver back in the skillet with enough gravy to just barely cover it. Now cover the top with sliced onion rings. Put a lid on it and simmer until the onions are done.

Serve with ketchup.

INLAND BEEF STEW

2 lbs. stew meat (cubed)	2 large onions (chopped)
4 large carrots (hunked)	1 toe garlic (crushed)
4 large potatoes (hunked)	¾ cup flour

In a large enough stew pot or dutch oven, fry down your meat in bacon grease until browned, and then add onion and fry until limp and you can see through them. Add the carrots, potatoes and garlic, cover with water, then salt and pepper to taste. Leave this on the fire and forget about it for a little while.

Now put the flour in an iron skillet and turn the stove on high. Push and stir the flour with a flat-ended spatula until it's deep brown but not burned. Then put it into the stew and stir until all lumps are gone. Cook the stew awhile and if it's too thick add a little water. If it's too thin cook it down until it's thick. When it's ready the meat should be tender and the vegetables falling apart. Serve over rice.

For *Coastal Beef Stew*, add a cup of stewed tomatoes, 3 bay leaves, ½ teaspoon of ground thyme, 2 more toes of garlic and a hot pepper. If you do this, you land up with a livelier stew.

Another variation is to use chicken stock instead of water, if you think the stew meat doesn't have enough flavor. Dana Kay Pullen said she discovered this by accident.

BRUNSWICK STEW

5 pounds beef	1 tablespoon of white sugar
5 pounds chicken	1 pod of hot pepper or
2½ pounds pork	1 teaspoon Tabasco®
5 pounds Irish potatoes	sauce (more if you
4 pounds of onions	want it real hot)
2 quarts of lima beans	2 bottles of ketchup
4 quarts of tomatoes	1 tablespoon of French's
2 quarts of Niblet corn	prepared mustard
1 quart okra	¼ teaspoon cloves
1 bottle of Worcestershire	¼ cup white vinegar
sauce (10 oz. size)	1 tablespoon of liquid
¼ teaspoon allspice	hickory smoke
6 Sunkist lemons (juice	1½ gallons of chicken-and-
only)	meat juice

Cook beef, chicken, and pork in pot covered with water until tender. Let cool. Grind in meat grinder. Grind the potatoes and onions; add to meat and juice. Cook 30 minutes. Add other ingredients as listed. Mix well. Cook 1½ hours, stirring often. If canning, cook only 30 minutes. Place in jars. Process 60 minutes at 15 pounds pressure or 90 minutes at 10 pounds pressure. If freezing, let cool, place in containers and freeze. Or serve hot with rice and corn pone.

Good for a family reunion or church supper.

AUNT ROSIE DEATON'S ALL-AMERICAN SLUM-GULLION
(The Best)

Cook some elbow macaroni — plenty. Brown minced onion (stronger the better), hamburger and/or bacon in a skillet. Add 1 can of whole Delmonte tomatoes, salt, pepper and all the macaroni you got. Simmer til you can't stand it any more, then take it off the fire and dive in. This is especially good when you're in a hurry-up day, like when there's a funeral, an auction, or a flag-burning at the Legion Hall.

CHILI

½ sack pinto beans, cooked
   until tender
2 onions chopped
1 bottle ketchup
1 pound hamburger meat

2 cans tomatoes
chili powder to taste,
   cayenne powder to
   taste, salt and pepper
   to taste

Cook pintos until tender. Brown meat and onions. Add to beans. Add tomatoes and ketchup and the other ingredients; cayenne, salt, and pepper to taste. Makes large dutch oven full.

JAIL-HOUSE CHILI

3 pounds diced lean beef
¼ cup Wesson oil
1 quart water
8 chili pods or 6
   tablespoons chili powder
3 teaspoons salt
5 cloves finely chopped
   garlic
1 teaspoon ground cumin

1 teaspoon marjoram
1 teaspoon red pepper
1 tablespoon white sugar
3 tablespoons paprika
To Thicken
3 tablespoons flour
6 tablespoons white corn
   meal
1 cup water

Heat oil in large pot, add meat and sear over high heat. Stir constantly until meat is gray but not brown. Add water and cover, cooking over low fire for 1½ to 2 hours. Add remaining ingredients, except for thickening, and cook at a bubbling simmer for 30 minutes. Add thickening which has previously been mixed with 1 cup of water. Cook about 5 more minutes, hand stir to prevent sticking. More water may be added if it's too thick. If meat is very fat, skim off fat before adding thickening. This is really hot chili.

CORN BEEF & HASH

1 can of corn beef	1 teaspoon of sugar
1 can of tomatoes	2 slices of fatback
3 medium potatoes (cubed)	1 bayleaf
1 large onion (chopped)	

Fry down onion and fatback til limp, then add potatoes and fry (stirring often) til brown. Add meat, tomatoes, sugar, and bayleaf. Salt and pepper to taste and serve over grits or rice.

"So good it'll make your tongue slap your jaw teeth out," says Edna Rae Mills.

SLOPPY JOE'S ON CORN BREAD

1 pound ground beef	¾ cup chopped onions
½ cup chopped bell pepper	½ cup chopped celery
1 grated carrot	1 No. 2 can Libby's
1 can tomato puree or	tomatoes
ketchup	¾ teaspoon salt
1 teaspoon black pepper	

Brown ground beef in big iron skillet. Stir in onion, bell pepper, celery, and fry until brown. Add carrot, tomatoes and puree. Stir mixture well, season with salt and pepper. Simmer for one hour and serve hot over hot-buttered cornbread. Serves 6.

"If you're using day-old cornbread, put it in a pie pan and use it for a lid while the Sloppy Joe's cooks. Everything'll be ready at the same time." — *Mildred Louise McQuaig.*

DIRTY RICE

1 lb. of ground beef   1 cup of rice
1 large onion (chopped)

Brown the ground meat and onions in bacon fat. Salt and pepper to taste. Add the rice covered with water, boil 1 minute while stirring. Put a lid on it and cook until the rice is fluffy and dry. About 25 – 30 minutes.

For *Spicy Dirty Rice* use 3 cloves of garlic, 2 peppers, ¼ pound chicken livers (chopped), 1 tablespoon Worcestershire sauce, a handful of green onions (chopped), and 2 tablespoons of parsley (chopped).

"After you've handled onions, get rid of that awful smell by rubbing lemon all over your hands." — *Eva Gay Ashworth, Pt. Neches, Texas.*

DANA PULLEN'S CHICKEN FEET & RICE

You can't get chicken feet at the supermarket these days,* so you gotta go to a butcher store and beg for them. (They're usually thrown away.) Once you get them, rinse them off, drop them into a pot of hot boiling water for five minutes and then take them out and the outer skin will just roll right off. Make sure you get it all off because there's no telling where the chicken's been walkin'. Now that the skin is cleaned off, take your cast iron dutch oven, cover the bottom with oil, put in the feet and fry til golden brown. Then put in a handful of chopped onions and one toe of garlic (flattened). Fry the onions until you can see through them, put in the desired amount of rice (depending on the number of people you're feeding), and cover with water. Salt, pepper, and bring to a boil. Put the lid on and cook the rice til fluffy and the chicken feet are tender.

The only way to eat a chicken foot is to gnaw on it. The round ball of the foot is the best part. They are a gristly kind of thing and can be used in soups, but when you fry them they're really good.

Serve with potato salad, greens, and biscuits.

Even though Miss Pullen says you can't find chicken feet in the supermarkets, we have talked to a lot of people who have seen them there.

SOUTHERN FRIED CHICKEN

You take a chicken and ya kill it
And you put it in the skillet
And you fry to a golden brown
That's Southern Cookin'
And it's mighty fine

According to Ernestine Mills, you take a good-sized chicken and cut it up the way you like it. Roll the pieces in salt and black pepper (plenty) and then roll it in flour until heavily coated. Heat grease (¼ cup bacon and ¾ cup vegetable oil) in a black iron skillet until a small bit dropped in jumps back at you.

Then put in enough chicken pieces to cover the skillet, but not too crowded. Fry it to a deep golden brown on one side and then turn it over. Lower heat til it simmers, and then fry that side to a golden brown. Takes about 35 minutes. Turn again if you see blood.

Serve with potato salad, rice, and chicken gravy made from the drippins (page 47).

SMOTHER-FRIED CHICKEN

Cut up one chicken; salt, pepper and flour it. Fry til golden brown in iron frying pan, remove it from the grease and make Mamma's Gravy (page 47). Then put chicken back in the frying pan with the gravy and smother for 20 minutes over medium heat.

If you have any Col. Sanders left over, make a gravy and throw it in. Smother for 20 – 30 minutes.

MARGIE'S FRIED CHICKEN

Cut up fryer, clean with lemon only. Dredge in a mixture of flour, salt, pepper, and allspice. Put in ½ inch of hot lard. Fry one side then the other until well done. Eat directly out of the skillet. This is very good with a cold beer. If you're a strict Baptist, have a lemonade or a cold drink, and may Gold bless your home.

PEARL'S CHICKEN & CORNBREAD DRESSING

Cook two pans of cornbread two days before you're going to fix your chicken and let it get hard in the refrigerator or on top of the stove. On the day your company's coming, you take a good fat hen and boil her down until you've got about three cups of rich chicken stock. Sometimes you need more, sometimes you need less.

Then, in a roasting pan, crumble up your two-day-old cornbread and mix with green onions all cut up, celery all cut up, boiled eggs all cut up, and some green pepper if you like it. All this is done to taste. Then add salt and pepper to taste and then add your boiled chicken, being careful to place her in the center of the pan. When she's positioned on her back you pour in the chicken stock, just enough to wet the cornbread if you like your dressing on the dry side, and if you like it on the wet side then you simply add some more stock. Next pop the bird (uncovered) in the oven (about 350 – 400) and when the dressing is hot through and through, or when it starts to bubble, take it out and start eating.

Serve with canned cranberry sauce, a green vegetable of your choice and sweet potatoes.

EVELYN WALTER'S NEVER-FAIL, SUNDAY BAKED CHICKEN

Take any old chicken. Clean with lemon only. Stuff; place in a baking dish or skillet; cover with a rag soaked in lard or Crisco. Bake at 275 degrees til tender and brown.

Stuffing: 2 cups dry bread, 2 cup chopped celery, 2 eggs, ½ teaspoon salt, ½ tablespoon pepper, 1 small package walnuts, 1 small chopped apple, 1 teaspoon of sage and a pinch of dry mustard. Pour drippins from baked chicken on stuffing mixture. Mix together and stuff. If not moist enough, add water.

"Don't turn the oven any higher or the rag'll catch on fire," says Evelyn, Kansas City, Mo.

CHICKEN STEW (WHITE)

1 chicken (cut for frying)
1 cup of chopped onions
1 cup of chopped celery
   corn starch or flour
    for thickening

salt and pepper to taste
2 tablespoons of bacon
   grease

In a dutch oven, heat the bacon grease and stir in the onions and celery. Fry them until they're limp but not beginning to brown. Add chicken parts and fry until the color has changed to white. Cover about 1 to 2 inches with water and cook until the meat is tender. Thicken if necessary. Serve over rice or make dumplings in the stew.

CHICKEN STEW (BROWN)

1 chicken (cut up)
1 bunch of green onions
   (chopped)
1 bunch of parsley
   (chopped)

¾ cup flour
½ cup bacon grease or oil
   salt, pepper, and Tabasco®
    to taste

Put drippins in a dutch oven and heat. Add flour and brown it to a rich brown, stirring constantly. Put the onions and parsley in the flour and add a little more oil if it's too stiff to stir. Cook a few minutes and add chicken parts and enough water barely to cover. Put in salt, pepper and tabasco to taste and mix everything real good. Put a lid on it and cook until the meat is just before leaving the bone. Serve over rice with corn and greens.

    This is very good with half-dollar-size dumplings made in the stew. You may need more liquid. If you do, just go ahead and add it.

MEMPHIS WOOD'S COVERED CHICKEN

Take some frying-size pieces of chicken. Salt and pepper them very good. Now smear with mustard until covered. Roll up each piece, individually, in tin foil and seal. Put 'em in a preheated oven at 400 degrees for 35 - 40 minutes.

Meanwhile, take out your corn for boiling, and your can spinach for heating, and your dinner's ready.

Serve the chicken in tin foil (2 or 3 per person). The kids will love unwrapping their own.

"I'd like to stress the point of being very generous with the French's mustard and when it's done, open it up and brown it under the broiler for an even more delicious flavor. Don't forget some Bisquick biscuits in that same oven, because they're as good as homemade. I use a lots of packaged things all the time, if they're good." — *Memphis.*

LORETTA'S CHICKEN DELIGHT

1 No. 14 can asparagus	2½ cups chopped cooked chicken
1 small can pimiento, chopped	3 hard-cooked eggs, sliced
¼ pound soda crackers, crumbled	1 can cream of chicken soup
½ soup can of water	¾ stick oleo

Place a layer of asparagus in bottom of greased casserole; add a layer of chicken, pimiento, eggs, and cracker crumbs. Repeat. Dilute soup with water; pour over casserole. Sprinkle with additional crumbs. Place slices of oleo over top. Bake at 375 degrees for 30 minutes.

ESTHER'S CHICKEN CASSEROLE MADE FROM SCRATCH

1 stewing hen
3 heaping tablespoons flour
1 onion, diced
3 tablespoons oleo or
   Wesson oil
½ teaspoon Calumet baking
   powder
   dash of curry powder
1½ cups sweet milk

6 – 7 cups salted water
   salt and pepper
2 cups diced celery
8 slices toast, diced
½ teaspoon poultry
   seasoning
2 eggs, slightly beaten
   dash of yellow food
   coloring

Cook chicken in water until tender; remove chicken from bone. Reserve 4 cups stock and add food coloring. Thicken reserved stock with flour. Season to taste. Place chicken in casserole; pour thickened stock over chicken. Brown onion and celery in oil, adding remaining ingredients. Season to taste with salt and pepper. Place on top of chicken. Bake at 325 degrees for 45 minutes to 1 hour.

FREDA'S FIVE-CAN CASSEROLE

1 small can boneless
   chicken
1 can cream of mushroom
   soup
1 can Chinese noodles
1 can chicken with rice
   soup

1 small can evaporated
   milk
1 small onion, minced
½ cup diced celery
½ cup sliced almonds

Mix all ingredients; place in casserole. Bake at 350 degrees for 1 hour.

LADY DIVINE'S CHICKEN-ASPARAGUS PIE

½ package dehydrated
    onion soup mix
1 can cream of chicken
    soup
1 cooked chicken, boned
    and cut into large
    pieces
¼ cup shredded Parmesan
    cheese

1 cup sour cream
2 pounds fresh-from-the-
    garden asparagus, or
    1 can cooked and
    drained
1 cup heavy cream,
    whipped

Add soup mix to sour cream; beat with rotary beater until well blended. Beat in soup. Arrange cooked asparagus spears cross-wise in a large, deep, heat-resistant platter. Spoon one-half the sauce over asparagus; cover generously with chicken pieces. Fold whipped cream into remaining sauce; pour over chicken. Heat at 350 degrees for 20 minutes. Sprinkle with Parmesan cheese. Place under broiler 5 to 6 inches from heat; broil til brown.

SPAGHETTI CHARLYSS

Add ¾ cup of good-grade, imported olive oil to a non-stick pot. Allow to heat over a medium flame for 2 to 3 minutes. Chop: 2 good-sized onions, ½ cup of parsley, 3 to 4 cups of pre-cooked ham, 1 stalk of celery, 4 good-sized cloves of garlic.

Add the chopped onions to the pot and stir thoroughly, allow to sauté for 2 minutes. Thereafter add the celery and parsley, stirring thoroughly. Allow these ingredients to sauté for about 7 to 10 minutes.

Add the chopped ham, 4 cans of tomato sauce, and stir thoroughly, mixing all the ingredients.

About 10 minutes into the cooking, add 2 tablespoons of grated cheese and stir thoroughly. At this time the addition of 4 or 5 good-sized bay leaves enhances the sauce's flavor.

Now add the finely chopped garlic to the cooking sauce. Allow everything to cook from 45 minutes to an hour, being careful to stir thoroughly every 2 or 3 minutes. After the hour's cooking is done, turn off the fire and let it sit for 10 minutes; then serve over a good-grade, boiled pasta. Serves 3 to 4 people.

ROSE'S SPAGHETTI CASSEROLE

1 ¾ cups raw spaghetti (all broken up)
¼ green pepper, chopped
¼ cup diced pimiento
¼ cup sweet milk
1 ½ – 2 cups cubed turkey, chicken or tuna

½ onion chopped
1 can cream of mushroom soup
½ teaspoon salt
⅛ teaspoon pepper
1 ¾ cups grated rat cheese

Cook your spaghetti and place it in a 2-quart casserole; add remaining ingredients. Bake at 350 degrees for 45 minutes.

"You can make a casserole out of anything. Throw your leftovers into an oven dish and mix with whatever you think will stick them together, an egg or some cheese maybe. Then bake til done." — *Betty Lou Hamilton, Groves, Texas.*

STEWED CHICKEN

2 cans Stokley's tomato sauce
4 bay leaves
2 tablespoons of brown sugar
1 tablespoon white vinegar

1 frying size chicken
1 can water
1 small onion, peeled and chopped
1 green bell pepper
2 tablespoons of oleo

Simmer onions and bell pepper in two tablespoons of oleo. Dump in tomato sauce, water, sugar, vinegar and bay leaves. Let cook slowly for 35 or 40 minutes. Stew chicken in another pan til tender. Pour mixture over drained chicken and simmer for 15 to 20 minutes and serve with rice, corn pone, and combination salad.

This is a coastal chicken stew. An inland one would not have tomatoes, bay leaves, brown sugar or bell peppers. It would be white and thick.

"If you follow the instructions on your pressure cooker you can cook a chicken til the meat falls off the bone in 20 minutes." — *Norma Jean Smith.*

LIVER-HATER'S CHICKEN LIVERS

1 lb. chicken livers	1 small bunch parsley
1 cup sweet sherry	1 cup cracker meal
1 small bunch green onions	salt and pepper

Cut the chicken livers into 1 to 1½ inch pieces. Put in a glass bowl. Add salt, pepper and ½ of the sherry, then let 'em soak for 30 minutes to an hour. Now chop your onions (green part and all) and parsley (not the stems) and set them aside.

When your livers are ready, roll them in cracker meal and fry in a hot skillet in ½ inch of grease. Turn them over a lot so they can brown on all sides. Then remove from skillet and pour off grease (but leave the drippins). Put onions and parsley in the skillet and fry for 1 minute. Now return the livers and add sherry. Simmer down for 15 minutes (or until the liquid is almost gone). You're guaranteed to like them even if you hate liver.

AUNT DONNAH'S ROAST POSSUM

Possum should be cleaned as soon as possible after shooting. It should be hung for 48 hours and is then ready to be skinned and cooked. The meat is light-colored and tender. Excess fat may be removed, but there is no strong flavor or odor contained in the fat.

1 possum	1 cup breadcrumbs
1 onion, chopped	1 hard-boiled egg, chopped
1 tablespoon fat	1 teaspoon salt
¼ teaspoon Worcestershire Sauce	water

Rub possum with salt and pepper. Brown onion in fat. Add possum liver and cook until tender. Add breadcrumbs, Worcestershire sauce, egg, salt, and water. Mix thoroughly and stuff possum. Truss like a fowl. Put in roasting pan with bacon across back and pour quart of water into pan. Roast uncovered in moderate oven (350 degrees) until tender, about 2½ hours.

There's only one thing to serve possum with — sweet potatoes. You only eat possum in the winter.

MAMA LEILA'S HAND-ME-DOWN OVEN-BAKED POSSUM

After you kill the possum be careful not to let him get away. While you're talking and planning how you going to eat him, he's going to be slipping right from under your nose. All he was doing was playing possum. Skin him and clean him before you go another foot, then the mess is gone and he won't get away. When you get him home, rub salt and pepper all over his body then run a mixture of vinegar and brown sugar over the salt and pepper. Wrap up the possum in a good baking pan and let it stand in the refrigerator overnight. The next morning, put the pan and let it stand in the refrigerator overnight. The next morning, put the pan with the possum still in it (hopefully) on top of stove. Add 2 or 3 spoons of bacon fat and sear him on all sides. Then add chopped onion (2 of them). Put in the oven and bake for 1 hour at 350 degrees. Pull him out and roll him over, and now you can add your sweet potatoes (just surround him with 'em). Put back in the oven and bake for another 1½ hours or until he is tender and juicy.

"Possum is tender and mild regardless of what other people think," Mama Leila say, "but you've got to watch 'em cause they'll slip away."

FRIED RABBIT

Cut up the rabbit into frying-size pieces. Soak it in vinegar and salt water (enough to cover) for about 1 – 2 hours. Take it out, pat it dry. Salt, pepper, and flour it. Put it in a hot skillet (with enough oil for frying) and fry until a rich brown and, when you stick it with a knife, you don't see any blood. Make gravy with the drippins.

BROILED SQUIRREL

Squirrel is one of the finest and tenderest of all wild meats. Its flavor is mild, rarely gamey. There is no need for soaking, and seldom any need for parboiling. They should be cleaned as soon as possible after shooting, but skinning may wait until they're ready to be cooked.

Clean squirrels and rub with salt and pepper. Brush with fat and place on hot broiling rack. Broil 40 minutes, turning frequently and basting with drippins every 10 minutes. Serve with gravy from drippins and season with 1 to 2 tablespoons of lemon juice.

FRIED SQUIRREL

Make sure all the hair is cleaned off the squirrel. Cut it up. If it's old and tough, put it in the pressure cooker for about 15 – 20 minutes.

Salt and pepper it. Cover with flour and fry in a cast iron skillet on a medium fire until brown and tender. This is a real sweet meat.

You can smother a squirrel just like a chicken.

BUTT'S 'GATOR TAIL

The only place you can find alligator is near the coast or the inland swamps in the South. So if you're lucky enough to get a holt to an alligator tail, there's a section about a foot long just behind the back legs that's tender and juicy. You cut it in sections at the joints just like you would a pork chop. Salt, pepper and flour each piece of tail and then fry in hot grease until golden brown. Or you can barbecue it with Bosie's Barbecue Sauce (page 49). He had alligator tail especially in mind when he concocted it.

If you haven't eaten 'gator tail before, you're in for a surprise. It's gonna taste a little bit like chicken, a little bit like pork, and a little bit like fish. It's so good, you'll wanna lay down and scream.

VENISON ROAST

Take a sharp knife and stick holes in the roast and stuff each hole with a sliver of garlic. The holes should be about 1 ½ – 2 inches apart like a pork roast. Then rub the roast with lots of salt and pepper. Flour it generously. Put in your dutch oven with ⅛ inch grease, and fry til golden brown on all sides. Put on the lid and cook *very slowly* until tender. No vegetables except potatoes, if you want them.

The meat should make its own juice, but if it doesn't, add a touch of white wine. NEVER add water to venison roast.

If you want to soak it overnight, some people do it in milk, some people do it in vinegar and salt water, and some don't do it at all.

MAMMA'S BROWN GRAVY

Leave enough grease in the skillet after frying meat (pork, beef, or chicken) and add 3 or 4 heaping tablespoons of flour on medium-to-high heat and stir constantly with a fork until dark golden brown. Then add water and cook until it just will run out of a spoon. Also, leave the crispies in the grease from the fried meat because they add a lot of rich flavor. Salt and black pepper to taste. Serve over hot rice, grits, or mashed potatoes.

YANKEE CREAM GRAVY

½ cup flour   salt and pepper
1 cup milk

To avoid lumps, put milk and flour in a jar and shake it vigorously until blended. After you have fried some green tomatoes, remove them from the pan and pour in the mixture of flour and milk. Stir constantly until it thickens and serve on top of the green tomatoes.

This will go with just about anything.

RED EYE GRAVY

After cooking the breakfast meat (bacon, ham, or sausage), remove it from the iron skillet and put it aside. To the drippins, pour ⅓ cup of strong coffee and stir while on the fire. Pour over hot grits or sop up with hot biscuits.

BOSIE'S BARBECUE SAUCE

(for all Meats, Fish and Fowl)

½ cup brown sugar
2 lemons
1 cup vinegar
3 cloves garlic
2 tablespoons ketchup
3 tablespoons mustard
   prepared
1 onion (chipped), large
3 strips bacon

2 tablespoons
   Worcestershire sauce
   (optional)
1 cup water
   pepper to taste
½ teaspoon salt
1 dash liquid smoke
   (optional)

Fry bacon until deep gold. Add onions and finish frying until they start getting brown. Add garlic and everything else in the recipe and bring to a boil. Turn fire down and simmer until sauce thickens.

Use on any meat for barbecueing.

(Tip) Rub the meat all over with brown sugar and salt and pepper.

Bosie said: "I smoked a number-three wash tub full of fish last week use'n this very sauce."

Fish, Cooter, 'n Shrimp

PERLOW

This is a rice dish unique to the coasts of North Florida, Georgia and South Carolina. It's like the Jambalaya of Louisiana; anything can be used to make it.

Shrimp Perlow

3 chopped onions	oil if needed
3 chopped toes of garlic	1 chopped bell pepper
1 cup of chopped ham, bacon, or salt meat	3 chopped ripe tomatoes or 1 can of stewed

Fry down onions, garlic and ham in a black iron pot that has a tight-fitting lid (but don't use it yet). When it's brown, add peppers and tomatoes. Simmer until tomatoes fall apart. Then add salt, pepper, tabasco, a good teaspoon of thyme, and 3 whole bay leaves. Add 2 cups of washed rice and cover with ½ inch of water. Bring to a rolling boil and drop in 2 or 3 lbs. of small, shelled shrimp. Stir them in, put the lid on, turn the fire to low, and cook until the rice is dry and fluffy. This is delicious with cold potato salad, especially if the perlow is peppery hot.

For a white perlow, put in chicken, pork backbones, or sausage with the onions and leave out the tomatoes.

For other good red perlows, use sausage, squirrel or chicken. And remember, shrimp is the only one that you add the meat to after you put in the rice. In the others the meat is put in with the onions to brown.

BETTER BAKED FISH

Soak 2 – 3 lbs. of King mackerel in:

2 tablespoons of ketchup	½ teaspoon sweet basil
2 teaspoons of vinegar	½ teaspoon sage
1 tablespoon of oil	salt and pepper
⅓ teaspoon curry powder	dash of garlic powder

After 2 or 3 hours (better overnight), remove fish from sauce and place on tinfoil. Spoon on some of the sauce and add ½ cup of cheap Sauterne. Then wrap tightly in tinfoil and bake at 400 degrees for 20 minutes.

When serving, spoon some of the uncooked sauce onto the hot fish.

FRIED CATFISH FILLET

For about 1 to 3 hours soak your catfish in 2 teaspoons of mustard, 3 or 4 tablespoons of canned cream, plus some salt and pepper.

Roll it in white cornmeal and fry to light golden brown in 1 inch of grease in a hot skillet. Catfish fries fast, so don't overcook it. It should be crispy on the outside and moist on the inside. If you serve it with anything else but hushpuppies, grits, cole slaw, and home fries, it'll get up and walk off the plate.

DAY-OLD FRIED FISH
(Cold & Pickled)

3 bay leaves	¼ cup of white vinegar
1 bunch of green onions chopped, or 1 medium yellow onion chopped	1 lime (use only the juice)
	3 tablespoons of ketchup
2 tablespoons of cooking oil	½ cup of stewed tomatoes
	salt to taste and pepper (tabasco) to taste
1 large clove of garlic, sliced	left over fried fish

Heat oil in iron pan. Fry green onions and garlic until limp. Add tomatoes and bay leaves and cook 15 minutes. Then add lime juice, ketchup, vinegar, salt and tabasco. Cook another 15 minutes.

Place cold fish in a deep dish in layers, and pour the above ingredients (hot) over the cold fish and let stand in refrigerator from 2 hours to 2 days. The longer you let it stand, the better the flavors.

Be careful of the bones.

SALMON PIE

2 eggs, beaten
1 teaspoon lemon juice
1 tablespoon chopped
   parsley
½ teaspoon pepper
½ cup buttered
   breadcrumbs

½ cup sweet milk
2 teaspoons chopped onion
½ teaspoon sage
1 1 pound can salmon,
   drained

Combine all ingredients in order given; place in 8-inch greased dish. Bake at 350 degrees for 40 minutes.

TUNA SALAD

1 can tuna
1 medium yellow onion
   (grated)
¼ cup hamburger pickles
   (chopped)
2 eggs (hard-boiled and
   chopped)
¼ cup celery (chopped fine)

½ apple, peeled and
   chopped larger than
   celery
black pepper
salt, if you think it
   needs it
½ – 1 cup mayonnaise

Mix all together and serve on toasted bread, or eat it on crackers. Good by itself, too!

FRIDAY'S TUNA FISH SALAD

1 can of tuna fish
½ medium yellow onion
   (finely chopped)
3 tablespoons of pickle
   relish

⅓ cup of mayonnaise
3 hard-boiled eggs
   (chopped up)
salt and pepper

Open your can of tuna fish. Turn it upside down (with the loose lid still on) and drain all the liquid out of the can. Dump it in a bowl. Add everything else and salt and pepper to taste.

If it's not juicy enough for you, add more mayonnaise. Serve on a leaf of lettuce or make sandwiches out of the bowl.

There's nothing better with tuna fish salad than potato chips, so make sure you've got a big bag for the folks.

FOUR-CAN DEEP TUNA PIE

1 can French-style green beans, drained	1 medium-sized can tuna
	½ can of milk
1 can of Campbell's mushroom soup	1 can of French-Fried onion rings, or a box
1 tablespoon of oleo	of frozen

Dilute soup with milk. Stir together beans, tuna, and soup. Bake at 400 degrees until bubbly. Top with onion rings. Put it back in the oven just long enough to make onion rings crispy. Serves 6.

CLARA JANE VICKAR'S CREAMED TUNA LUNCH

Brown 2 tablespoons of flour and 3 tablespoons of butter or oleo in a skillet. Add the tuna (big can is best) chunk style and 1 small container half-and-half or 2 cups of milk. Cook over low heat til thickened. Salt, pepper, and serve with toast or rice. Carnation evaporated milk is good in this, too.

COOTER PIE (THE HUNTER'S DELIGHT)

First you take a live cooter and wait for him to stick his head out from under his shell. When he does, you grab it and whack it off. Take a hatchet to the underside so you can get to the meat and remove it along with the liver, tripe and eggs (if he has any?). Set aside.

½ cup of chopped bacon	1 stewed tomato, chopped
2 medium onions, chopped	1 teaspoon of thyme
2 toes of garlic, crushed	¼ cup of flour

Fry all the above down until it's brown, then add the cooter and continue to cook. It's best in a black iron dutch oven. Don't forget to salt and pepper it to your taste.

Brown the flour in an iron frying pan. Stir constantly to avoid burning. But make sure you brown it good. Then add it to the cooter with enough water to make it soupy. Stew down til meat is falling off the bone and the liquid is thick.

Now make biscuit dough and drop small-sized biscuits over the top of the stew. Stick it in a preheated oven at 400 degrees and bake done (golden). A hunter will come out of the woods to get this!

MOCK COOTER SOUP

3 pounds lean beef or ground meat	1½ quarts of water
1 pint sweet milk	¼ pound of oleo
1 tablespoon flour	½ pint cream
½ teaspoon mace	2 hard-boiled eggs cut up
½ teaspoon dry mustard	in medium-size chunks

Boil meat and water until one quart of liquid remains. Add one pint of milk and ¼ pound oleo. Remove meat, allow to cool, grind, and return to stock. Let it cook down a little more. Add flour dissolved in cream. Add seasoning.

Miz Ina also says: "To make a real one just add cooter meat instead of ground meat. That's the way we do it in Sandfly, Georgia."

SUPERIOR SHRIMP (MISSISSIPPI)

2 lbs. of shrimp, shelled (but leave tails on)	2 toes of garlic, chopped
½ cup of chopped bacon	1 cup of stewed tomatoes
1 small onion, chopped	2 bay leaves
	salt and pepper to taste

Fry down the onions and garlic and bacon. Then cook the shrimp, rolling them in the onions til they curl up. Now add the tomatoes, bay leaves, salt and pepper. Stew about 10 or 15 minutes and let stand for a while before serving hot over a great old big pile of rice. Betty Sue accused Raenelle of stealing this recipe out of some fancy book but she still swears she got it at a high-priced restaurant while she was on vacation in Shell Beach, Miss.

MRS. ARNOLD'S SATURDAY NIGHT SHRIMPS

In a big piece of cheesecloth, tie up 3 bay leaves, 2 cloves of garlic, one minced onion for each pound of shrimp, 2 lemons (sliced), and 2 dried peppers. Boil shrimp spices in a big pot of water for 15 minutes. Dump unpeeled (but headed) shrimp in, and boil them for ten minutes. Then remove the shrimp and set aside. Pour out half the water in the pot, remove spice bag, and add juice from a large jar of Heinz's sweet pickles. Then, cook the liquid down some more. Return the shrimp to this juice and chill for about 4 hours. Drain. Serve with the sweet pickles left from the juice, crackers, and ketchup. Let everybody peel their own.

SHRIMP AND EGGPLANT CASSEROLE

2 eggplants
1 medium onion, chopped
1 medium bell pepper,
   chopped
1 cup celery, chopped fine
   red pepper, paprika,
   garlic, salt
2 lbs. shrimp

2 cups slightly undercooked
   rice (measure after
   cooked)
1 can buttered, toasted
   crumbs
½ lb. sharp cheddar cheese,
   grated
¼ cup vegetable oil

In a heavy iron skillet over a medium fire, fry shrimp in the oil, stirring lightly until they are pink. Remove shrimp from skillet and fry onions, celery, and bell pepper until tender but still crisp. Add to shrimp.

Peel eggplant, cut in cubes, cover with slightly-salted water, and let simmer until tender, but not too soft. Drain well, add salt and pepper, then mix rice, eggplant and shrimp mixture. It should be highly seasoned (pepper). Stir lightly and spoon into a 2½ quart buttered casserole. Pour undiluted can of cream of mushroom soup over top of mixture, then grated cheese. Lastly, add the buttered, toasted breadcrumbs. Sprinkle with paprika, place in pre-heated, 350-degree oven for 25 minutes. Serves 8.

This recipe is from the table of Father Bob Landry, St. Alphonse Catholic Church, Maurice, La. He always says "They got more, cher!"

CRAB STEW OR CLAM CHOWDER

3 tablespoons of bacon fat
2 large onions (chopped)
3 toes of garlic (sliced)
1 large can of stewed
   tomatoes or 2 cups of
   home-stewed
3 bay leaves

4 – 5 medium potatoes
   (cut up)
1 dozen fresh crabs (still
   wiggling), or frozen
1 cup of crab meat
1 teaspoon of thyme
   salt and pepper to taste

Put onions, garlic, and bacon fat into a hot skillet and fry until golden. Add the tomatoes, juice and all, and cook it down until all the liquid is gone. Pour this into a stew pot and add the potatoes, bay leaves and hot peppers. Cover with the water, add salt and pepper and simmer on medium fire until the potatoes are tender.

Meanwhile take the shells off the crabs and remove the devils fingers (the pointed things). Do not remove the legs. Now, chop the bodies in half and crack the claws with the handle of the knife. When the potatoes are tender, tump the crabs (bodies and claws) and the crab meat into the stew. Add thyme and more water if needed. Cook twenty more minutes and serve over rice.

You can thicken this with ½ cup of skillet-browned flour (dry) right after you put the crab meat in.

Clam Chowder: It's exactly the same except use clams instead of crabs. It takes 3 cups clam meat, fresh or canned (chopped).

SHEBA SPANN'S MOCK SHE-MOCK CRAB STEW

Get a whiting fish, or any flaky white fish, and put it in a pot of water and with a little salt. Bring to a boil. When the fish begins to come apart, stop, drain and skin. Then flake the meat til it looks like crab meat. Now hard-boil 4 eggs so you can use the yolks *only*.

2 tablespoons of oleo	1 pinch of allspice
1 small onion (minced)	2 cups of mock crabmeat
4 cups of sweet milk	(whiting)
1 tablespoon of flour	salt and Tabasco® to taste
mock crab eggs (hard-	(plenty)
boiled egg yolks)	some dry sherry (plenty)

Fry the onion in the oleo until it is limp. Add milk and let it heat but do not *boil*. Stir in the flour and the allspice. At the very last minute add the mock crab meat and season the stew. Let it sit for about 10 minutes before serving. Sprinkle the mock crab eggs on the top of the stew after it is in the bowl and just go ahead and drink the sherry.

Sheba says: "You can fool the best of them."

KLEBERT'S COLD CRAWFISH SOUP

1 medium onion	2 cups milk
2 tablespoons butter	1 cup thick cream
2 white potatoes	tabasco, celery salt, and
2 cups chicken broth	pepper, to taste
1½ teaspoons salt	1 – 2 lbs. crawfish tails

Mais cher, if you don't stay to South Louisiana, you fish market probably won't have crawfish, mais shrimp will do.

Brown you onions in butter; add you potatoes (sliced thin), broth, and salt. Bring to boil, cover and simmer for thirty minutes. Puree in you 'lectric mixer and then add you cream and season. Add half you crawfish or shrimp and puree again. Add you other crawfish tails or shrimp whole and cool in you ice box 'til real cold. Serves 6 – 8 of you best hungry friends.

Dinner Salads
'n Sweet Salads

COMBINATION SALAD

1 head iceberg lettuce   3 medium-size tomatoes
                                 (ripe)

Rinse your lettuce and chop into 2-inch pieces (bite-size). Clean your tomatoes and cut them up into 1-inch squares.

Combine the tomatoes, lettuce and enough mayonnaise to generously coat everything. Then salt and black pepper to taste and tumble some more. If more moisture is needed, add a spoon or two of white vinegar.

"It's so good with fried chicken or pork chops and is enough to feed a whole family," says Betty Sue, "and there ain't no secret to makin' it."

LAURA LEE'S FRESH SUMMER SALAD

2 cucumbers   2 medium-sized tomatoes
                      (ripe)

Take your cucumber and cut off the ends. Then with an end in one hand, the cucumber in the other, rub together real hard and fast. When the liquid starts to foam, stop. Now peel and slice them.

Meanwhile, slice your tomatoes and place both the cucumbers and tomatoes in a long, low, Pyrex baking dish, and cover with cider vinegar, and salt and pepper to taste. Chill for ½ hour before serving. Delicious with field peas or black-eyed peas.

HAM-LIMA SALAD

Chop your four hard-boiled eggs. Cut two cups of ham into ½-inch cubes. Add two cups of drained, cooked green lima beans, one cup of chopped celery, 1 tablespoon finely chopped onion, ½ cup Blue Plate mayonnaise, ½ teaspoon curry powder, salt and pepper. Mix, taste for salt, chill an hour or more to blend flavors. Then help your plate!

MONA LISA SAPP'S MACARONI SALAD

4 cups of elbow macaroni
(cooked and drained)
½ cup mayo
3 – 4 tablespoons sweet
pickle relish
¼ cup onion
(finely chopped)

1 small jar of pimientos
(chopped)
2 tablespoons light
salad oil
1 teaspoon French's
mustard
salt and pepper to taste

Put everything together in a big bowl and mix it very good. If you need more juice, add a spoon or 2 of vinegar and re-mix. This goes very well with fried foods (hot or cold). It's enough for a tableful.

To this recipe you can add either 1 cup of cubed cheese, 1 can flaked tuna, 1 cup fried ground meat (cold), or 1 cup of chicken meat (cooked and chopped).

Mona says: "You can turn this salad everyway but loose and it's gonna be good!"

REBECCA VENERABLE'S SAUERKRAUT SALAD

1 large can sauerkraut
1 onion (medium)
1 green pepper
½ cup celery

jar pimientos
½ cup vinegar
½ cup olive oil
1 cup sugar

Chop onion, pepper, celery, pimientos, and also chop sauerkraut. Mix all ingredients together and let stand two days before eating.

RICE SALAD

2 cups cooked, chilled rice
½ cup chopped king crab
   or lobster
½ cup slivered Virginia ham
½ cup finely chopped celery
2 finely chopped
   hard-boiled eggs
   salt and freshly ground
   pepper

1 tablespoon chopped
   chives
¼ cup chopped parsley
1 tablespoon olive oil
1 tablespoon wine vinegar
½ cup Blue Plate
   mayonnaise

Combine by tossing lightly the rice, crab, ham, celery, eggs, chives, and parsley. Sprinkle with oil and vinegar. Add mayonnaise and season. Let stand in the ice box for a few hours for still better flavor.

AUNT CORA'S COLESLAW

1 medium head of
   cabbage
1 medium yellow onion
   (chopped)
½ pint of mayonnaise (use
   more if you want it
   juicy)

3 heaping tablespoons of
   pickle relish (a little
   juice)
salt and pepper

Shred and chop that cabbage head until it's as fine as you like it, and then put it in a bowl. To the bowl, add your onion, mayonnaise, pickle relish, salt and pepper to taste. (Black pepper is very important to a good coleslaw.) Now let it stand in the ice box for 2 or 3 hours before using.

This is perfect for a big fish fry with hush puppies, home fries, and grits. (Page 54).

ANGEL FLAKE AMBROSIA

6 – 8 oranges (peeled and
    cut up)
4 – 5 bananas (cut into rounds)
  1 bag Angel Flake coconut

1 medium-size jar of
   maraschino cherries
   (with juice, cut in half)
1 – 2 cups of sugar to taste

Mix all the fruit together and add sugar, cherries, and coconut. Put in the refrigerator and serve ice cold. It should be good and juicy. Christmas wouldn't be Christmas without it, and it's even better if you let it set til New Year's.

SURPRISE SALAD

½ cup cold water
3 envelopes plain gelatin
5 cups applesauce (2 No.
   2 cans)

¼ cup red cinammon candy
½ cup white sugar
½ teaspoon nutmeg
2 tablespoons lemon juice

Put your gelatin in a bowl; add your cold water and dissolve it. Heat candy and applesauce in a pan on medium heat until it bubbles. Then you add your gelatin. Then add all the other ingredients. Then pour the mixture into a mayonnaised mold. Now you chill it til it's firm; and then you unmold it and garnish with parsley or anything green.

"Even Reba get jealous when I make this," says Stella Carlisle of Eclectic, Alabama.

FANNIE'S FIVE-CUP SALAD

1 cup of little
  marshmallows (white,
  not colored)
1 cup of Angel Flake
  coconut

1 cup of canned mandarin
  oranges (drained)
1 cup Libby's fruit
  cocktail (drained)
1 cup of sour cream

Combine all these ingredients in a large glass or Tupperware bowl. Cover; place in the ice box for two hours or overnight. May be served as a salad or dessert. Nuts and cherries (canned) may be added.

    Mrs. Fannie Paulk, of Evening Shade, Ark., says: "It'll dress up any occasion, it's so fancy!"

FRUITED SOUR CREAM SALAD (BANANAS)

6 bananas (firm and not
  too ripe)
1 pint of sour cream or
  imitation

1 cup of brown sugar
1 teaspoon of cinnamon
1 can of mandarin oranges
½ teaspoon of nutmeg

Slice bananas and add drained mandarin oranges in a bowl. Mix sour cream, sugar, cinnamon, and nutmeg. Pour over bananas and oranges. Mix and chill.

FRUITED SOUR CREAM SALAD (WHITE GRAPES)

2 lbs. seedless white grapes
1 pint of sour cream or
   imitation

1 cup brown sugar
1 teaspoon cinnamon
½ teaspoon of nutmeg

Wash grapes and pick from stems. Mix sour cream, sugar, cinnamon, and nutmeg. Pour over grapes and chill. (You can cut your grapes in half if you want to.)

Jinny Beaufort Houseworth says: "These are both flavorites at every brunch in Ty Ty, Georgia!"

For brunch these are delicious with scrambled eggs, grits and sausage.

LUCY'S GUARANTEED STEWED PRUNES

1 lb. box of prunes
½ cup of sugar

1 lemon (sliced)

Dump your prunes in a pot and cover with cold water. Put them on the fire and bring to a slow and easy boil for 15 minutes.

Now add your sugar and lemon and cook for 15 minutes more. Remove from the fire and cool. Serves 8.

Delicious with cheese dishes, and good for you too.

Sandwiches 'n Eggs

KISS ME NOT SANDWICH

Spread mustard on two pieces of bread. Then slice onion on one and cover with the other. Ice tea helps wash it down.

ANOTHER KISS ME NOT SANDWICH

2 slices of bread
  (wholewheat)

peanut butter
sliced bermuda onion

Spread on the peanut butter and place on the slices of onion. Put them together and eat. You'll need a drink with this.

CANNED CORN BEEF SANDWICH

Butter two pieces of bread with mayonnaise (generously). Cover one with sliced corn beef and bread 'n butter pickles. Top with the other piece of bread. This is delicious with a Cocola!

ANTI-STICK PEANUT BUTTER SANDWICH

Butter one slice of bread with peanut butter, then butter the other side with mayonnaise (generously). Put them together and eat (will not stick to roof of your mouth — partials not included).
  Delicious with glass of cold milk.

POTATO CHIP SANDWICH

2 slices of bread   potato chips
mayonnaise

Spread the mayo generously across the bread. Pile the potato chips on to one of the slices as high as you can. Then top it with the other slice and mash down until all the potato chips are crushed.

Pardie Tickette says: "Wash it down with a Pepsi, it's some good!"

PAPER-THIN GRILL CHEESE

2 slices of Velveeta cheese   2 slices of white bread
(no other will do)   (no other will do)

Heat your iron skillet with a pat or two of butter in the bottom. Put your slices of Velveeta cheese between the 2 slices of bread. Now place it in the hot skillet. With a turner, mash and toast the cheese sandwich on both sides until the cheese is melted and the bread is toasted. (The flatter the better.)

KITCHEN SINK TOMATO SANDWICH

In the peak of the tomato season, chill 1 very large or 2 medium tomatoes that have been vine-ripened and have a good acidy bite to their taste.

Take two slices of bread. Coat them with ¼ inch of good mayonnaise. On one piece of bread, slice the tomato ¼ inch thick. Salt and pepper that layer. Add another layer of sliced tomato, and again salt and pepper. Place the other piece of bread on top of this, roll up your sleeves, and commence to eat over the kitchen sink while the juice runs down your elbows.

FRIED EGG SANDWICH

Spread two slices of bread with mayonnaise. Put the fried egg (soft or hard) between them after you've salted and peppered it.
    Sometimes this is the only way you can eat breakfast.

CHARLOTTE'S DEVILED EGGS

You hard-boil your eggs, cut 'em in half, longwise, and then take the yellow and toss it out. Throw in some Hellman's mayonnaise, pickle juice, lemon juice, celery salt, and celery seed (that's the secret). Mash all this up well and then stuff it back into the whites; and, if you want to be fancy, put a dash of red or black caviar on top.

RICE AND EGGS

1 cup used rice	salt to taste
5 eggs	pepper to taste
⅓ cup milk, cream, or sour cream	1 squirt of Tabasco®

Beat eggs, milk, salt, and pepper. Pour in medium-hot greased skillet. Stir til eggs start lumping together, then add rice. Cook until they're the way you like them. Serves 3 or 4.
    "When you're scramblin eggs, always add a little milk or cream to make them lighter and go further," says Barbara Jean Hubbard, Mill Creek, Alabama.

Tabasco is a registered trademark of the McIlhenny Company

IDA'S INDIAN ONION CURRY OMELET

1 tablespoon of vegetable oil

6 – 7 eggs

3 green scallions

1 teaspoon of curry powder

1 teaspoon prepared mustard (French's yellow)

½ cup of milk

Fry sliced green onions in medium-hot skillet. Add mixture of eggs, milk, curry, mustard, and salt and pepper to taste. Cook until eggs are firm and all liquid is gone. Serves 4 or 5.

Serve with toast and plain sardines, cold.

Ida Dillard, of Due West, South Carolina, said: "You got to be kinda wild to try this one. It weeds 'em out."

LEETTA'S FANCY EGGS & CHEESE PIE

4 whole eggs

1 cup of chopped parsley

1 cup of Swiss cheese, grated

½ teaspoon of nutmeg

½ pint of whipping cream

1 unbaked 9-inch pie shell

Mix eggs, cream, nutmeg, salt, and pepper. Pour into pie shell that has been baked for 5 minutes at 400 degrees. Sprinkle in cheese and parsley and bake for 25 minutes at 350 degrees or until brown on top.

Mrs De Wald says: "This ain't our dessert, it's for a light supper or brunch."

OOZIE'S OKRA OMELET

1 cup of fresh okra, cut in rounds

½ cup chopped scallions

6 – 7 eggs

⅓ cup of milk

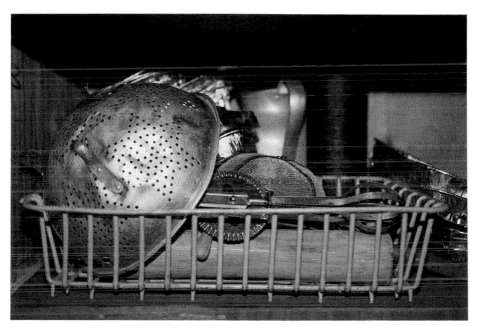